W9-DDT-542

Personal Fighting Gear

STEPHANIE FITZGERALD

Heinemann Library
Chicago, Illinois

© 2004 Heinemann Library,
a division of Reed Elsevier Inc.
Chicago, Illinois

Customer Service 888-454-2279

Visit our website at www.heinemannlibrary.com

Series designed by Heinemann Library
Page Layout by Malcolm Walker
Photo research by Bill Broyles
Printed and bound in China
  by WKT Company Limited.

08 07 06 05 04
10 9 8 7 6 5 4 3 2 1

Library of Congress Cataloging-in-Publication Data

Fitzgerald, Stephanie.
  Personal fighting gear / Stephanie Fitzgerald.
    p. cm. -- (U.S. Armed Forces)
Includes bibliographical references and index.
  ISBN 1-4034-4553-2 (hardcover) --
ISBN 1-4034-4559-1 (pbk.)
 1. United States--Armed Forces--Equipment--Juvenile
literature. 2. United States--Armed Forces--Uniforms--
Juvenile literature. 3. Military paraphernalia--United States--
Juvenile literature. [1. United States--Armed Forces--
Equipment. 2. United States--Armed Forces--Uniforms. 3.
Military paraphernalia. 4. Military uniforms.] I.
Title. II. Series: U.S. Armed Forces.
  UC523.G73 2004
  355.8'0973--dc22

                    2003023802

Produced for Heinemann Library by
White-Thomson Publishing Ltd
2/3 St Andrew's Place
Lewes UK   BN7 1UP

Acknowledgments
The author and publisher are grateful to the following for
permission to reproduce copyright material
pp. 1, 7R, 13 Joe Raedle/Getty Images; pp. 3, 16, 33 Scott
Nelson/Getty Images; p. 4 Jim Hollander/AFP/Corbis; pp. 5,
11, 12T, 32, 45T U.S. Marine Corps; pp. 6, 7L, 8, 9, 12B,
19B, 25, 26, 30, 31, 35B, 36, 37 Defense Visual Information
Center; p. 10 Aaron Favila/AP/Wide World Photos; pp. 14,
44C Library of Congress; p. 15 Robert Nickelsberg/Getty
Images; p. 17 Klepper; pp. 18, 19T, 23, 45B Military Stock
Photography; p. 20 Erik S. Lesser/Getty Images; p. 21 Randy
White/US Air Force/KRT; p. 22 Reuters/Corbis; pp. 24, 27,
35T U.S. Navy; pp. 28, 29 James A. Sugar/Corbis; p. 34
Dave Martin/AFP/Corbis; pp. 38, 40, 41 U.S. Air Force;
p. 39 James A. Sugar; pp. 42, 43 U.S. Coast Guard; pp. 44B,
45C Corbis; p. 44T National Archives and Records
Administration
Cover courtesy of the Defense Visual Information Center

Special thanks to Lt. Col. G.A. Lofaro for his review
of this book.

Some words are shown in bold, **like this.**
You can find out what they mean by looking
in the glossary.

Contents

Body Protection

The United States Armed Forces are made up of five **branches**: the army, navy, air force, marines, and Coast Guard. Often the branches work together. Air force bombers and fighter pilots, for example, fly in front of the army to attack the enemy.

Each branch of the **military** has different units to do different jobs. The navy has sailors that work on destroyers, submarines, and **aircraft carriers.** It also has pilots who fly fighter jets, tankers, and bombers.

All members of the military have personal fighting gear such as **small arms** to do their jobs. But sometimes soldiers need special gear to do a specific job.

Body armor

Combat soldiers in the army and the Marine Corps wear the Interceptor Body Armor (IBA). This is a vest made of a special fiber called Kevlar® that can protect against small arms. It has another piece to protect the soldier's neck. Small plates made of strong boron carbide (a tough ceramic material) can be put into the vest for more protection. These plates are called Small Arms Protective Inserts. The IBA can protect a soldier from **shrapnel**, 9 mm pistol bullets, and 7.62 mm rifle bullets.

Know It

The caliber of a weapon refers to the size of its bullets. It is a measurement of the bullet's diameter, or how wide it is. Caliber can be given in inches or millimeters. For example, a .223 caliber bullet is 223 thousandths of an inch (in.) in diameter, which is equal to 5.56 millimeters (mm).

This marine is wearing a helmet and has a camouflaged flak jacket over his uniform with a flag tucked in it.

Headgear

Helmets used to be made of steel. They were very heavy. Steel helmets could protect a soldier's head from falling objects. They could even be used for cooking! But the helmets could not stop a bullet. Since the 1980s, soldiers have used a different helmet made of Kevlar® and plastic.

The helmet is a lot lighter than steel, and it is five times stronger. The Kevlar® helmet can stop a bullet from a .22 caliber weapon, such as a handgun or rifle. There is a place on the helmet where soldiers can attach earphones and a microphone so that they can talk to each other. Night vision equipment can also be attached to the helmet. Protective gas masks can be worn with all Kevlar® helmets. This helps a soldier breathe safely when there is poison gas in the air. The helmet can also hold a plastic face shield or goggles.

These soldiers are wearing protective headgear— their Kevlar® helmets.

Camouflage: Hiding in Plain Sight

Soldiers are safer if the enemy cannot see them. It is also important to hide equipment, trucks, and tanks. That is why camouflage is so important.

Camouflage uses colors and patterns to hide a person or equipment. The colors used on soldiers' clothes match the area around them. Sometimes camouflage materials use just one color. Other times they use patterns with many colors. These kinds of patterns make it hard to see the outlines of the soldiers. They blend right into the trees, shrubs, and shadows around them.

Know It

Soldiers use different colors to blend into different areas. In the desert, soldiers wear uniforms with sand and light green patterns. In places covered in snow, they wear white and a light tan color (called loam). In areas with trees such as the jungle, they wear light green and loam uniforms.

To blend into the trees, these marines are wearing camouflaged uniforms and skin paint, and they have branches stuck in their helmets.

Battle uniforms

Soldiers wear three things when they get ready to fight: camouflage **fatigues** called BDUs (for Battle Dress Uniforms), a helmet, and boots. Each soldier adds different equipment to this basic uniform for different activities.

BDUs are made of material that will not rip and can dry very fast. The pants have button flies instead of zippers. That is because zippers can get stuck if they get wet, muddy, or sandy. The pants also have huge pockets for carrying extra gear. Straps on the waist can be pulled tight to make the pants fit better. Straps on the cuffs make it easier for soldiers to tuck their pants into their boots.

White uniforms are used as camouflage by soldiers in snowy areas. In desert areas, soldiers wear light-colored, spotted uniforms.

Marine BDUs

For twenty years soldiers in the army, air force, and marines all wore the same BDUs. But recently, the marines started wearing their own special camouflage uniforms. Instead of being "blobs" of color, patterns on the new uniforms are made of groups of tiny squares. These patterns help a soldier blend into the background faster than regular BDUs. The new uniforms also have a small marine **insignia.** They make the marines stand out from other troops.

Camouflage netting, paint, and screens

Soldiers also need to camouflage their helmets. Soldiers in World War II (1939–1945) put netting on their helmets. This kept the sun from shining off the steel helmet. Soldiers could also stick branches and leaves in the netting. The helmets used today are covered in the same material used to make BDUs.

Camouflage is not used only on clothing. Soldiers also use paint and equipment screens. They even use natural materials found in their surroundings, such as branches and grass, to hide themselves and their equipment.

The netting over this Bradley infantry fighting vehicle keeps it hidden from airplanes.

Hiding Vehicles and Ships

When equipment is not being used, soldiers cover it with camouflaged netting or screens. Vehicles are also camouflaged by being painted. As with uniforms, trucks can be camouflaged with one color to match the area, or with a pattern that uses different colors. In the past, even navy ships were camouflaged. The ships were not painted to match the water, though. They were painted with a colorful pattern so enemy submarines could not tell the front of the ship from the back or in which direction it was sailing. Today, this is no longer done.

This soldier paints his face with the colors used in jungle areas.

Using paint to hide

Soldiers also camouflage their skin. Skin reflects light. This can catch the enemy's attention. Soldiers paint their skin in patterns like the ones on their uniforms. Areas that stand out more, such as cheekbones, chins, noses, and ears, are painted in a dark color. Areas that are shadowed, like around the eyes and under the nose and chin, are painted in a light color.

Soldiers have to paint all the skin that is not covered by a uniform. That includes the back of their necks, their arms, and hands.

Other Ways to Hide

There are other ways soldiers can hide. When an enemy is nearby, soldiers must stay very still and be very quiet. They should also hide shiny objects, such as a **compass** or watch. Soldiers are also taught never to look up if they hear a plane flying overhead. Soldiers' upturned faces are the easiest things to see in a photo taken from an airplane.

If soldiers do not have camouflage paint, they may have to use natural camouflage. They use materials found in the area like burnt cork, bark, charcoal, or mud. Soldiers only use mud when there is no other choice, though, because it contains germs.

The Army Infantry Gears Up for Battle

The infantry is just one of many army units. These troops are sent in for up-close fighting with the enemy. They use camouflaged fatigues and helmets to stay out of sight. They also use an assault rucksack, or backpack, to carry food, water, supplies, and a first aid kit.

The food that soldiers used to carry was called combat rations. The rations were usually meals like meat and vegetable stew or hash. Rations came in a can that looked a lot like dog food. They did not taste much better! Today soldiers carry Meals Ready to Eat (MRE). These MREs contain the main meal, a snack, dessert, and a drink. They also have a flameless heater so soldiers can have a hot meal. To heat their food, soldiers put their meal pouch into a heating sleeve and add water. The heating sleeve contains chemicals that produce heat when mixed with water. The meal is hot in just about 15 minutes.

A plastic-wrapped precooked Meal Ready to Eat (MRE) contains meat loaf, potatoes, pastry, cocoa, and coffee.

Useful Chewing Gum

Since World War I (1914–1918), chewing gum has been included in combat rations. Chewing gum can help keep soldiers' mouths moist and their teeth clean. It can also help them stay calm and ready for action. Ford Gum & Machine Co. supplies the 72 million pieces of gum that are packed into MREs each year. Army gum has to stay fresh for three years. But how the Ford gum lasts so long is a mystery. The ingredients are a secret!

Protective clothing

Chemical and biological warfare means using poison gases or germs against enemy troops. Troops carry a gas mask so that they can breathe clean air at all times. In an emergency soldiers put on their masks and then put on their helmets over the top of the mask.

It is hard to tell who is who when soldiers are wearing overgarments. That is why they wear a piece of tape on their arm with their name on it.

When troops are in areas where there may be a threat of chemical attack, they wear Battle Dress Overgarments (BDOs). The BDO is a charcoal-lined coat and pants. Just as the charcoal filter in a kitty litter box keeps the smell from getting out, the charcoal filter in the BDO keeps chemicals from getting in. The BDO is worn with a mask, specially treated rubber gloves and liners, and chemical protective overboots.

Know It

During Operation Iraqi Freedom in 2003, soldiers got equipment from home. There is no water in the desert. Soldiers did not get showers. Baby wipes were their secret weapon for keeping clean. The wipes were also good for taking off camouflage paint.

Good communication

Staying in touch is a very important part of **combat**. In the past, soldiers had to shout to each other and use hand signals. Today, they use high-tech headsets.

This soldier is using a headset to talk to another soldier.

There are three headsets a soldier can take into combat. The RA-3185 Cobra Modular Infantry Radio headset looks just like the hands-free microphones that pop stars use. The microphone blocks out everything but the soldier's voice. The earpiece sits a little bit away from the ear. Soldiers can listen to what is being said and still hear what is going on around them. Soldiers riding in noisy vehicles use the RA-108 Headset or the RA-315 Integrated Helmet System. Both block out noise so that soldiers can hear what people are saying to them.

Seeing in the Dark

When soldiers need to see in the dark, they use night vision goggles. The goggles can be held, strapped to a soldier's head, or attached to a helmet. The goggles have lenses that make everything look a lot bigger, just like a magnifying glass. They also have an infrared spotlight lens. Goggles with infrared lenses give off an invisible beam of light. Only the person wearing the goggles can see it. That is how soldiers can see in the dark.

This soldier has his night vision goggles pushed up onto his helmet.

Infantry weapons

An important part of fighting is having the right weapons. There are a lot of weapons for a soldier to choose from. The different weapons soldiers use depend on what they are trying to do. A piece of fighting gear that they always carry, though, is a rifle.

During World War II, soldiers carried the M1 Garand semiautomatic rifle. The Garand could fire eight quick shots. It was twice as fast as any other rifle. But the rifle had two problems. When it was fired, the Garand jerked back very hard into the soldier's shoulder. This is called a kickback. When the clip, or **ammunition** supply, was empty, it made a loud "ping" noise as it flew out of the gun. This sound let the enemy know the soldier had to stop shooting to reload.

Since 1963 soldiers have carried a Colt M16 rapid-fire weapon into battle. It can fire 700 to 950 rounds (or bullets) per minute and only weighs 7 pounds (3.18 kilograms). The M16 is a very accurate weapon. That means soldiers will always hit their target as long as they are aiming right! Each soldier also carries a night vision scope and a grenade belt that holds up to six grenades.

This soldier carries his M16 and a belt of ammunition around his chest.

Scopes

Scopes, or sights, help soldiers aim their guns. The scope attaches onto the rifle. When the soldier looks through the scope, the target looks closer. It works just like a telescope. Some scopes also have crosshairs. These are very thin lines that cross in the middle, like a plus sign. A soldier's aim is perfect when the target is in the center of the crosshairs. Other scopes have a red dot in the middle. The soldier has to line up the dot with the target for a perfect shot.

Cavalry Scouts: Reconnaissance Equipment

At the beginning of a mission, cavalry scouts are sent ahead of the infantry. They use **stealth** and **surveillance** to get information. Sometimes they also capture the enemy. This is called **reconnaissance**. They try to find out what the area is like, where the enemy is, and how many troops are there. Then they pass the information, called **intelligence,** back to the infantry.

Cavalry soldiers used to travel on horseback. Today, scouts travel three different ways. They use helicopters to gather information from above. This is called aerial reconnaissance. On the ground they use armored personnel carriers, tanks, and cavalry-fighting vehicles. Scouts also travel on foot to get very close to an enemy position.

Mountain bikes

Scouts recently got a new vehicle — mountain bikes. A bike makes it easier for a soldier to move quickly and quietly through rough areas. The bikes are even used by **paratroopers**. They can be dropped from a plane. When they are not being used, the bikes can be folded up.

Cavalry During the Civil War

Cavalry soldiers in the Civil War (1861–1865) looked very different from today's scouts. They rode horses over rough ground, so their uniforms included boots, spurs, and heavy gloves called gauntlets. Civil War scouts either wore a standard cavalry cap (called a kepi) or—in sunny areas—a Western-style hat that kept their heads cool. Cavalrymen carried a .52 caliber Sharps carbine. Since some of their fighting was done on horseback, they also carried the United States Army Model 1850 saber. This sword was so heavy and long that soldiers called it the Old Wrist Breaker!

A Union Army cavalry officer and his horse relax before a battle.

Dragon Eye

Sometimes it is too dangerous to send a scout out for information, such as when troops are on one side of a hill and do not know what is on the other side. For times like these, the military is creating tiny flying vehicles for surveillance. The first, Dragon Eye, fits in a backpack and is put together like a model plane. It is only four feet wide. It has a global positioning receiver, which tells troops exactly where it is. It also has a video camera and radio transmitter so troops can see and hear everything the Dragon Eye does.

A soldier prepares a Dragon Eye for flight over Tahrir, Iraq, a day after the city was captured in March 2003.

Communications gear

If scouts cannot report what they see as soon as they see it, their entire mission could be ruined. **Communications** equipment is some of the most important fighting gear that scouts use.

Today's scouts use the Computer/Radio Subsystem (CRS). This system can send messages over great distances, and it is easy to carry. There are no wires on the CRS. A camera sits right on the soldier's gun. The leader has two radios with a flat panel display—like the screen on a laptop computer. Now everything scouts see and hear can be passed right on to commanders.

For times when scouts come face-to-face with the enemy, they carry the M16 rifle. They also carry M203 grenade launchers, M60 machine guns, and antitank weapons. Antitank missiles, such as the Javelin, can shoot right through armor.

Army Green Berets: High-Tech Gear

There are times when a battle cannot be fought using regular troops. Then, small units with soldiers who have different fighting skills are used. These troops might be used for fighting in thick jungles, or on secret missions. Such battles need to be fought without anyone finding out what has happened.

This type of fighting takes special kinds of soldiers, such as the men in the Army Special Forces. These soldiers, called Green Berets, are usually asked to perform special **reconnaissance** and rescue missions.

This Green Beret is firing an M4. See how the used bullets fly out of the gun.

Foreign Troops and Weapons

Green Berets are also called force multipliers. A big part of their job is to train friendly foreign troops. A team of 10 to 12 Green Berets can train 300 to 500 local soldiers. Special Forces also have to know how to use foreign weapons, like the Russian AK47 assault rifle, the German G3 assault rifle, and the Israeli UZI submachine gun.

Technicians prepare a Klepper kayak for a demonstration.

Special Forces missions

Most Green Beret missions are top secret. The soldiers have to make sure they are not caught going into or leaving an enemy area. Like other members of the armed forces, the Green Berets use camouflage. They also move around as quietly as possible.

Special Forces soldiers can **infiltrate** an area in a lot of different ways. Most of the time, they enter a target area by parachute. Other times they enter from the water. For this, they use the Klepper folding kayak. A kayak is one of the quietest ways to travel over the water. Kyaks do not have motors. Careful paddling lets the Green Berets glide over the water without making a sound.

In the water, the Klepper can carry two Green Berets and hundreds of pounds of equipment. Once on land, the kayak can be taken apart in just five minutes. It weighs only 80 pounds (36.29 kilograms), so one person can carry it.

Ranger Beads

Special operations soldiers use Ranger beads to keep track of how far they have walked. The string of beads is easy to carry. It can be hung around the soldier's neck or worn on a belt or uniform. There are two sets of beads on the string. One set counts off every 100 meters traveled. The other counts every 1,000 meters traveled.

Green Beret teamwork

Green Berets work in twelve-man teams. The team has two officers. They are the leaders. The team also has two operations and **intelligence** sergeants. They gather information and help plan the team's actions. There are also two weapons sergeants, two **communications** sergeants, two **medics**, and two **engineers**. Having two of each type of soldier means the unit can break into two teams that can work on their own.

Know It

Semiautomatic weapons fire one bullet at a time. After each shot, the gun is made ready to fire again. With a semiautomatic weapon, the used bullet pops out of the gun. A new bullet loads by itself. The shooter has to pull the trigger again. But a fully automatic weapon, like a machine gun, keeps firing until all the ammunition is gone.

One of the weapons carried by each team is a .50 caliber **semiautomatic** rifle. This gun uses big **ammunition**, like the bullets used in a heavy machine gun. It is better than a heavy machine gun, though, because it is light. The gun weighs less than 30 pounds (13.6 kilograms).

The teams also carry the M16A2 rifle. When a weapon has extra letters and numbers after it, like *A2,* that means some changes have been made to the gun. Two team members change their rifles by adding **grenade** launchers. These can be attached under the barrel of the gun. The launchers can shoot a grenade up to about 450 yards (400 meters). That is longer than four football fields!

This Green Beret has an M16A2 with a grenade launcher attached.

A Green Beret sees a green scene such as this through his night vision goggles.

Working in the dark

Sometimes Green Berets work in the dark. Each member of the team has a set of night vision goggles. Like all of their gear, the Green Berets' goggles are the most powerful. The soldiers can see faraway objects even when there is no moonlight.

As hard as it is to see in the dark, it is even harder to hit a target in the dark. For this, Green Berets use laser aiming lights on their guns. The laser shoots a beam of light along the barrel of the gun and marks the target with a dot. Green Berets use a special laser aiming light. It shoots a beam that can be seen only with night vision goggles. This way the enemy cannot see where the soldier is aiming.

Naming the Green Berets

In 1961 President John F. Kennedy visited Fort Bragg, North Carolina. Kennedy was interested in a different kind of warfare. He felt that the new Special Forces soldiers were the perfect people for the job. They had been wearing green berets since 1953 to set themselves apart from other military units. With Kennedy's support, it became the official headgear for Army Special Forces soldiers, and they became known as the Green Berets.

Green Berets wear their their dress uniforms for special events.

Army Rangers: Portable Gear

The Rangers are a unit of the United States Army's special operations forces. They fight the enemy up close and handle special missions. They go on recovery missions to rescue people who are in danger and perform **reconnaissance** and security missions. They may also conduct forced entry missions, such as taking over an enemy airfield.

Surprising the enemy is very important if a special mission is going to work well. Rangers need to get into the enemy's territory by land, sea, or air. Since the Rangers are an **airborne** unit, they usually use parachute jumps or fast rope insertion.

Getting on the ground quickly

Fast roping is the quickest way to get a lot of troops on the ground. With fast roping, Rangers travel by helicopter. To leave the helicopter, Rangers slide down a three-inch nylon rope. They wear gloves to protect their hands from rope burn and a helmet and goggles to protect their heads and eyes.

Army Rangers fast rope from a Blackhawk helicopter.

Fast Rope Braking

Rangers use only their hands as a brake on the rope. They never use their feet. Braking with the feet would wear out the rope. This makes it dangerous for the Rangers who come afterward. Soldiers use their hands to brake by gripping the rope tightly and turning their hands in, as if they were wringing a towel.

Rangers use static line parachute jumps to put a lot of soldiers into an area quickly.

Fast roping is quick, but it is also very noticeable. To get in secretly, Rangers need to drop from higher in the sky. For this, they use a High-Altitude Low-Opening parachute system. Parachutes in the sky are easy to see from the ground, so Rangers **free-fall** for as long as possible. Then they open their parachutes close to the ground.

High-altitude jump gear

There are problems with jumping from very high in the air. It is very cold up there, and there is not a lot of oxygen. If the Rangers do not get enough oxygen, they could faint. Rangers use special equipment for high jumps. Their parachutes have an automatic ripcord-pulling device. If the Ranger free-falls past a set height, the device opens the parachute. The Ranger needs a helmet, goggles, gloves, and an oxygen bottle and mask.

Delta Force

Terrorism has become a serious problem in the world. The United States. government has special units that fight terrorists. The most famous one is Delta Force. Delta Force is in charge of getting back planes that have been taken over by terrorists. They are also in charge of rescuing Americans who are in trouble in other countries. Delta troopers have all the best weapons and equipment. A lot of their gear has been made just for them. Delta Force is mostly made up of soldiers who were already in special operations, such as Rangers and Green Berets. The government, however, keeps most of the details about Delta Forcesecret.

Easy-to-carry gear

Rangers are called a rapid deployment force. That means they must always be ready to move anywhere in the world within 18 hours. All of their weapons must be easy to carry. Rangers have regular army uniforms and weapons, such as the M16. But as a special operations team, they also carry very special weapons.

Many Rangers carry the M4 carbine instead of an M16. It is a lot like the M16, except it is shorter and is lighter to carry. It also has an extra handgrip in the front so a soldier can hold on with both hands while firing. The M4 has a special sight that helps soldiers aim. When they look through the sight, a small, red dot appears where the bullet will hit.

Volunteering for the Rangers

The 75th Ranger Regiment is one of America's top units, and it is not easy to get into. Soldiers in the 75th are **volunteers.** First, the soldiers volunteer for the regular army. Then they volunteer to go to **airborne** school to learn how to jump out of planes and helicopters. If soldiers pass airborne training, they can volunteer for Ranger school. If a soldier gets into an actual unit after graduation, there is still more training with the unit.

This soldier is using an M4 rifle with a sight attached.

Rangers can also attach special equipment to the M4. This can include a **grenade** launcher, other kinds of sights, and a sound suppressor that allows the gun to be fired without making much noise.

Sound Suppression

When a bullet is fired, it creates sound waves. The sound of a gunshot is made by those waves. A sound suppressor works just like the muffler on a car. The suppressor is shaped like a tube. The inside is filled with rubber or metal mesh disks. When the gun is fired, the sound waves bounce around on the disks inside the suppressor until they run out of energy. The noise that finally comes out is more like a "pop" than a "bang." It is not correct to call a sound suppressor a silencer. A suppressor only lowers the noise; it does not get rid of it completely.

A suppressor can be attached to a semiautomatic pistol.

Navy Gear: At Sea or on Land

When most people think of the United States Navy, they think of big ships and submarines filled with sailors. That is right, but it is not the whole story. The navy also includes fighter pilots and SEALs—the navy's special operations force.

Sailors on board navy ships are not armed. Because they are on a ship and not in up-close fighting, their uniforms are very different from the ones ground troops wear. They do not need camouflage. The navy has a lot of traditional uniforms that they have been using for more than 200 years. The master-at-arms is the only sailor who wears camouflage. There is not any military reason for this. It is just a navy tradition. The master-at-arms is also the only sailor who carries a **sidearm**—usually a pistol.

Know It

The master-at-arms is in charge of keeping peace on the ship. Small ships might have one master-at-arms. **Aircraft carriers**, with 5,000 people on board, are just like a floating town. They have 65 to 70 masters-at-arms on board.

A flight deck crew scrubs the deck. These sailors are wearing their everyday uniforms.

Jerseys Indicate Jobs

Flight crew sailors who work on the deck of an aircraft carrier wear different-colored jerseys depending on their job. This helps pilots know who does different things. For example, pilots look to sailors in yellow jerseys for directions. These are the crew members who move the planes around the flight deck and launch them. Sailors in red jerseys work with weapons and load bombs onto planes. Purple shirts (called grapes) are in charge of fuel.

A flight deck crew in different-colored jerseys spreads out a crash barrier.

Everyday uniforms

A sailor's work uniform, the one worn every day, is a pair of blue pants and a light blue shirt. An officer's work uniform is khaki pants and a shirt. Sailors and officers wear their dress uniforms only for special occasions. The dress uniforms for sailors are blue jumpers in winter and white jumpers in summer. This outfit is what most people picture when they think of a navy uniform.

Flight deck uniforms

Sailors who work on the flight deck of an aircraft carrier wear a different uniform. The flight deck can be a very dangerous place when aircraft are taking off and landing. A crew member could get blown overboard by the force of a jet engine. So these sailors wear safety equipment. Their jerseys are **inflatable**. They are called float coats. If someone falls overboard, the shirt fills with air and keeps the sailor above water. They also wear heavy-duty helmets, called cranials, to protect their heads. It can get pretty loud on deck, so the helmets come with cups to protect the ears. Goggles on the helmet protect the eyes from blasts of air from the jets.

Navy SEALs: Underwater and in the Sky

SEALs are the navy's special fighting force. SEAL is short for SEa Air Land teams. SEALs get into **hostile** areas in many different ways. For a long time, SEALs traveled over water using the combat rubber raiding craft. This **inflatable** boat is also called a Zodiac boat or "rubber duck." It can be tossed out of an aircraft.

Two of the SEALs in this Zodiac boat are ready to dive. They are wearing wet suits.

RHIBs

Today SEALs usually use rigid-hull inflatable boats (RHIB). They are mostly made of fiberglass, so they are very stable and solid. Only the upper edge of the ship's side, called the **gunwale**, is inflatable. The smallest RHIB is 24 feet (7.3 meters) long. When it is fully loaded, it weighs about 10,000 pounds (4,535 kilograms). A radar system and a machine gun can be mounted on board.

Unusual Transport

SEAL teams need to get in and out of an area without being noticed. Special operations forces call this leaving a "small footprint." If a team cannot get in by water, SEALs will use any way they can find. They use military vehicles, motorcycles, and even sports cars.

Tiny Subs

A SEAL Delivery Vehicle (SDV) is a tiny submarine that carries soldiers to shore. The SDV can move faster than a swimmer and can travel farther. Lights from inside the SDV would give away its location, so there are no windows. Since the pilot cannot see, he has to use computer systems to steer. It is also a wet ride. Passengers wear full diving gear because they are surrounded by water for the whole trip. A new Advanced SEAL Delivery System (ASDS) is being tested in Hawaii. It has a dry chamber and can be launched from a submarine.

An SDV is being driven into the water

Gear for arriving underwater

When SEALs approach the land from underwater, they usually wear a standard wet or dry suit. A wet suit is a tight rubber suit that divers wear to stay warm. A wet suit traps water between the suit and the diver. The water gets warmed by the diver's skin and does not leave room for new, cold water to get inside. Divers in wet suits look a little like real seals! A dry suit is made of waterproof material. It traps warm air between the diver and the suit. A diver in a dry suit does not get wet.

SEALs who are swimming underwater cannot come up for air. They have to use air tanks like people who dive for fun. These are called scuba tanks. But these tanks are noisy and they cause a lot of air bubbles to rise to the surface. SEALs have to be quiet and invisible. They use a type of air tank called the LARV. It does not release the diver's breath into the water, so there are no bubbles.

Sometimes SEALs just swim ashore. During these surface swims, they use an Attack Board, or Compass Board. The board is made of plastic and has a **compass**. This helps the SEAL figure out which direction he is swimming in. The board also has a watch and a depth gauge. This gauge tells the SEAL how deep the water is.

Parachute jumps

Sometimes SEALs jump out of a helicopter into the water with a Zodiac boat. For parachute jumps, they have three choices: static line, High-Altitude High-Opening, and High-Altitude Low-Opening.

On some missions SEALs use static line drops. This is the easiest way to reach the ground quickly with a lot of gear. A line is attached to the soldier's parachute pack and to a cable in the plane. When the SEAL drops, the line pulls the parachute open. For these jumps, SEALs use a round parachute with a reserve parachute. The reserve parachute opens if the main one fails. Soldiers wear camouflaged jumpsuits and helmets. They also carry a strobe light or flares for signaling and safety gear such as goggles, gloves, a knife, and a life jacket.

For High-Altitude High-Opening jumps, a SEAL uses a square parachute. The front of the parachute has little openings. Since the back is closed, air gets trapped underneath the parachute and keeps it in the air. The SEAL only **free-falls** for eight to ten seconds before the parachute opens. Then he glides toward the ground. He pulls ropes on either side of the parachute to steer.

SEALs glide through the air in their High-Altitude High-Opening parachutes.

A SEAL sometimes has to wear full diving gear while carrying underwater weapons and bombs.

SEAL firepower

All special operations forces have good equipment. But SEALs get the prize for the strangest weapon—a pistol that fires underwater. The gun shoots darts and can fire ten in a minute. The weapon works on batteries and can even be reloaded underwater. Any other information about the gun is top secret!

SEALs use a lot of different weapons on land. The carry the same M16 as other troops, but they attach a **grenade** launcher to theirs. They also use an MP5N submachine gun. The MP5N fires 800 rounds per minute. It is mostly used for fighting in small spaces.

Shotguns are also good for close fighting. They are more reliable than **semiautomatic** guns. The semiautomatics can jam in damp and dirty conditions. When a gun jams, it cannot be fired. SEALs also carry pistols. On top-secret missions, they put sound suppressors on their guns and use subsonic ammunition.

Quieting Gunshots

Part of what causes the loud noise from a gunshot is the sonic boom. That is the noise a bullet makes when it breaks the sound barrier. (That means the bullet is moving through the air faster than sound travels.) Subsonic ammunition is made with less gunpowder than usual. This way, the bullet never even reaches the speed of sound. There is no sonic boom. When used with a sound suppressor, subsonic ammunition makes hardly any noise at all.

The Marines: Equipped to Take on Anything

The United States Marine Corps is part of the navy. Marines usually travel on navy ships, but they work in the air, on land, and at sea.

All marines get the same basic equipment, starting with their All-purpose Lightweight Individual Carrying Equipment, or ALICE pack. In its frame, this giant backpack is wider than the soldier carrying it! When it is full, the ALICE pack weighs about 100 pounds (45.34 kilograms). Soldiers waterproof their packs and cover them with a camouflage cover.

Marine Packs

When soldiers are going to be on duty for a few months, they have to carry everything they will need in their packs. An ALICE pack has a large storage area for things like a tent, sleeping bag, mosquito netting, extra clothing, and an extra pair of boots. It also has six pouches on the front,

Marines on their way to Afghanistan carry MOLLE packs and M16A2 rifles.

where a soldier can keep food, night vision goggles, headsets, and personal items. The new Modular Lightweight Load-carrying Equipment (MOLLE) pack is smaller and less bulky than the ALICE. It can hold 25 pieces of equipment, two hand **grenades,** two canteens, and 180 rounds of **ammunition.**

A hospital corpsman prepares an ALICE pack before going on an exercise.

Essential extras

One thing that all marines have in their packs is a first-aid kit. It is very important that any injury gets treated right away, even if it is only a cut or scrape. Marines also carry a poncho shelter and entrenching tool. If soldiers are outside in bad weather, they can take cover under the poncho. The entrenching tool can be used to dig a hole or a trench to hide from the enemy.

All soldiers also carry a canteen, a cup, and a cover. These simple pieces of equipment are important to a soldier's survival. Soldiers need plenty of clean water to drink, especially if they are in the desert. Canteens were once made of tin. Today's canteens are made of plastic. They come with a filter that removes chemicals, germs, and even bugs!

Marine Corps weapons

Weapons used by marines include a 9 mm service pistol and the M16A2 rifle. The rifle can come with a bayonet. A bayonet is a blade attached to the muzzle of a rifle. (The muzzle is the end of the gun, where the bullet comes out.) When a bayonet is attached to a rifle, it can be used like a spear. A marine uses a bayonet when the enemy is too close for a rifle. Soldiers also use a bayonet if they run out of **ammunition**. Marines carry hand **grenades**, too.

A yellow smoke grenade is used to mark a landing zone for helicopters.

Grenades and Their Use

Soldiers use different grenades for different reasons. A fragmentation hand grenade sprays metal pieces into the air as it explodes. Chemical smoke hand grenades are used as signals. The smoke screen created by these grenades can also hide troops. This is called providing cover. An incendiary grenade is used to destroy equipment or just to start a fire. *Incendiary* means something that can cause a fire. An offensive/concussion grenade creates shock waves in the air. Some shock waves are so strong that they can destroy buildings.

Cooling the Weapons

When a weapon is fired, the gunpowder inside the bullet burns. That burning powder heats up the gun's metal barrel. The heat disappears as it passes into the air around the gun. Then the gun's metal cools down. That is called air-cooling. This happens in most guns. But air-cooling is most important for automatic weapons. These guns fire so fast that they create a lot of heat. And there is not much time between rounds for the gun to cool. This could cause the barrel to burn out. That is why these guns have holes or other openings in the barrel. They let more heat move to the surrounding air more quickly.

Crew-shared weapons

Weapons like rifles and pistols are individual gear. Soldiers all carry a rifle or a pistol of their own. Some weapons are shared by an entire unit. An example is the belt-fed, air-cooled M240G machine gun.

The ammunition for an M240G is made up of a lot of bullets. They are attached to each other on a long belt. The belt of bullets is fed through the gun while a soldier shoots. The soldier does not have to stop to reload very often.

A soldier fires the M240 while his partner helps feed the belt of ammunition.

Aviators: Gear for Fliers

Pilots can be found in every branch of the armed forces. They fly fighter jets, **navigate** bombers, or lead search-and-rescue teams. Most weapons that pilots need are part of their plane or helicopter. The most important equipment pilots use is safety gear. All pilots wear the same basic equipment: a flight helmet and a flight suit.

The flight helmet and suit

A flight helmet protects the pilot's head. It also has a headset attached so pilots can talk to their crews. The helmet also includes a visor with dark or clear lenses. The visor can be lowered over the pilot's eyes or raised up on the helmet. It can also have night vision goggles. The helmet has a place for an oxygen mask. A tube runs from the mask to the airplane's oxygen system. The oxygen mask has a microphone so the pilot can talk to the crew.

A pilot's flight suit is made of **fire-retardant** material. It has a lot of pockets and storage areas. What an aviator carries in the pockets changes from mission to mission. Many pilots carry a checklist, charts, and maps. All pilots also carry personal identification in case they land in enemy territory during combat.

Preflight Check

One thing that might be on a pilot's checklist is a preflight check to make sure all of the plane's equipment is working. If the pilot has bombs on board, the checklist is a reminder about when to drop them. The checklist also has emergency procedures. Every pilot memorizes **"boldface"** procedures. "Non-boldface" procedures do not have to be memorized.

Navy pilots, equipped with flight helmets and visors, head for their planes.

A pilot with a harness over his shoulders is buckled in and ready to take off.

Buckling up

The first thing a fighter pilot does when he or she gets into the **cockpit** of the airplane is buckle up. Every pilot wears a harness. The harness attaches like a seat belt to the ejection seat and a parachute.

G-force gear

Fighter pilots sometimes fly in ways that create G-forces, or gravity forces. This happens when a pilot goes into a dive, flies straight up very quickly, or makes sharp turns. Pilots call this "pulling Gs." They measure it in numbers such as "One G" or "Two Gs." One G-force equals the weight of your body. Two Gs is twice your weight. So when pilots feel one-and-a-half G-forces, they feel as if they weigh one-and-a-half times their normal weight.

A pilot gets his flight suit tested.

Pulling Gs can be dangerous. Pilots can lose their vision. This happens because the pilot's blood has rushed away from the brain and lungs. The pilot could also pass out. That is why fighter pilots wear G-suits. The suit covers the pilot's waist and leg area. It has pouches of air at the stomach, thighs, and calves. When a pilot is feeling G-forces, the air pouches **inflate**. This presses down on the muscles and forces the blood to keep flowing toward the lungs and brain.

Survival gear

Fighter pilots also wear a survival vest. The vest has a pocket that fills with air as soon as it touches water. This keeps the pilot from drowning. If the pocket does not **inflate**, the pilot can pull on two ropes that will blow it up. The pilot can also blow up the vest through a tube. It works just like the life vest on a regular airplane.

The survival vest includes three rescue items. There is a portable radio to send voice messages and Morse code. Morse code combines different lengths of sound or light to make different letters in the alphabet. For example, one short sound or flash plus one long sound or flash (. _) equals the letter *a*. The vest also has a dye marker. When the marker is broken open, the dye spreads through the water and turns it bright green. This makes it easier for search-and-rescue crews to find the pilot. The vest also contains flares that can be used during the day or night. One end of the flare creates a flame; the other gives off a smoke signal.

Know It

Pilots wear their flight suit, harness, and helmet every time they get into a plane, even when they are not in combat. The only piece of equipment they add during combat is a 9 mm handgun. If pilots are flying on a night mission, they might also carry night-vision goggles.

An air force pilot wears his life preserver jacket while inspecting a dummy missile on his plane's wing.

Survival kit

The cushion of the ejection seat also includes a survival kit. Inside are a raft, a water purification kit, a survival knife, and fishing equipment. These come in handy if the pilot has to wait a while to be rescued. The kit also includes a signaling mirror and a whistle. The kit can include other equipment, as well. Pilots pack different gear for different missions. If the pilot is planning to fly over a cold area, things like long underwear and heavy socks would be added to the survival kit.

A helicopter pilot in helmet and visor goes over his checklist before taking off.

Helicopter Pilot Gear

Helicopter pilots use some of the same equipment as other pilots. But helicopter pilots do not deal with G-forces. They do not wear a G-suit. Helicopter pilots do not wear a harness, either. That is because they do not have ejection seats or use a parachute. Ejection seats work by blasting up and out of the aircraft. It would be impossible for a helicopter pilot to eject past the helicopter's blades. In an emergency, pilots do a "hover down," or crash landing.

Air Force Special Operations Field Gear

Different air force units do different jobs. Air Force Aerospace Expeditionary Forces (AEFs) are made up of fighters, bombers, tankers, and **tactical** airlift. These units keep enemy planes away from where they are not allowed. They also go on rescue missions and carry out air strikes. Pilots use the same gear as other aviators. The air force also has a special operations force, called Special Tactic Units (STs). These units are made up of Combat Weather Teams, Combat Control, and Pararescue.

Combat Weather Team

It is important to know what the weather will be when planning an attack. If a sandstorm is coming, a mission might be delayed. Rangers might want to wait for a cloudy night to start a secret mission. The Air Force Combat Weather Team helps special operations decide when to plan a mission.

Know It

Combat Weather Teams are well trained. They have to get into dangerous areas quickly. They have passed **airborne** training and can jump out of planes and helicopters. Team members are trained to dive, too. Members carry an M9 pistol and an M4 assault rifle.

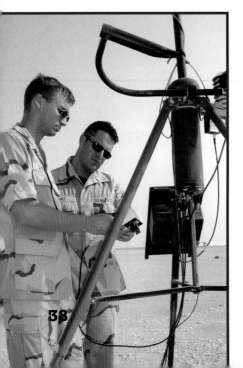

The Combat Weather Team uses the Tactical Meteorological Observing System (TMOS) to get information. The TMOS weighs only 216 pounds (98 kilograms). The system uses sensors to test the air. The TMOS measures wind direction and speed. It also measures the temperature, and can tell if it is going to rain, snow, or sleet. The system can measure the height and layers of clouds. It can even sense lightning 25 miles (40 kilometers) away.

Weather specialists set up an observation system.

Members of Combat Control use a SOFLAM to mark a target.

Combat Control Team

The Combat Control Team uses surveying equipment to help special forces set up targets and find drop zones. Drop zones are areas where planes can land or drop troops and supplies.

The surveying equipment the controllers use is a lot like that used by road construction crews. But the controllers' equipment is smaller and easier to carry. One controller can set up an entire airfield.

To measure distances, surveyors use a laser range finder. It looks like a small video camera. The controller points the range finder at an object and pulls the trigger. The range finder shoots a laser beam that hits the object and reflects back. This tells the controller how far the object is and if an area is suitable for plane landings, for dropping supplies, or for landing helicopters. The controller also has to figure out where the drop zone is. To do this, a Global Positioning System (GPS) receiver is used. When the receiver is turned on, satellites send back information to the receiver telling where that spot is on Earth.

"Painting Targets"

Combat Control also "paints targets" in enemy areas. They do not really use paint, though. The controller uses lasers to mark the spot that bombers should aim for. The Special Operations Forces Laser Marker (SOFLAM) measures the distance to a target and marks it with a laser dot. The controller gives the target's location to a pilot. Then the pilot drops a laser-guided, "smart bomb" programmed to hit that laser mark.

The controllers sometimes have to be armed. Most carry an M6 rifle. The M6 is an M16 with a night vision scope and targeting equipment. But the controller's most important piece of equipment is a radio to communicate with pilots, commanders, and the rest of the team.

Pararescue: Life-Saving Gear

Pararescue Units, called PJs, are the air force's special rescue and medical team. They are trained to give medical care in emergencies. They also rescue pilots and other special operations units that are trapped in enemy lands. PJs use any way possible to reach troops in trouble. They are trained in parachute and helicopter drops and underwater operations.

Regular military medics are called "noncombatants." That means they do not fight, and they do not carry weapons. It is against the law to shoot at a medic or take one hostage. PJs are combatants. Like other special operations units, pararescuers are a well-trained fighting force. A PJ comes under attack almost every time he goes on a rescue mission. For this reason, PJs carry the M6 rifle.

A Special Parachute Suit

PJs get a lot of parachute training. They practice for emergencies during training so that they are ready if an emergency really happens. They train for when their parachute does not work, or when they get tangled in trees. Sometimes, when they go on real jumps, PJs wear the Parachutist Rough Terrain System. This padded suit protects a PJ's neck, armpits, kidneys, elbows, crotch, and knees.

This PJ has his Parachutist Rough Terrain System on.

A PJ (on the right with pack on back) helps a soldier get pulled to safety.

Medical supplies

Another important piece of equipment PJs carry is the ALICE pack. The pack is filled with medical supplies. PJs never know what they will face when they reach an injured soldier. So they carry anything they might need. Their packs are usually filled with the same supplies found in an ambulance, such as bandages, painkillers, **splints**, and **tourniquets**. The only difference is that PJs have to carry the 100-pound (45.3-kilogram) packs on their backs.

Off-Duty Pararescue

When they are not on duty, PJs help out in disasters such as earthquakes, floods, or tornadoes. After the 1989 earthquake in San Francisco, California, PJs were there to help. Miles of highway overpasses had fallen. Many drivers were trapped under piles of concrete. The area was very dangerous. The concrete kept moving and falling. People were afraid to rescue the drivers. PJs **volunteered** for the job. Their motto is "That others may live."

The Coast Guard: Gear for Patrolling Harbors and Coasts

The Coast Guard is somewhat different from other military branches. The Coast Guard is active, or working, during war and in peacetime.

The Coast Guard patrols harbors and coasts. It also protects other ships and equipment on the water. The Coast Guard's most important equipment is its boats. It uses large boats, called cutters, and smaller patrol boats.

Stopping Illegal Immigration

One of the Coast Guard's major duties is to stop illegal immigrants from entering the country. Illegal immigrants try to get into the United States without permission. The Coast Guard does not treat these people like criminals. It considers these missions humanitarian operations. That means doing something to help other people. Some of the immigrants are running away from conditions in their own country. Some are afraid to go back. The Coast Guard usually takes these people from small boats and rafts onto its own boats and tries to get them help.

A Coast Guard petty officer on lookout carries an M16.

During Operation Iraqi Freedom, the Coast Guard was there to enforce UN sanctions against Iraq. Iraq was not allowed to ship oil out of the country. The Coast Guard had to board Iraqi ships to make sure they were not sneaking out any oil. Since sailors were going onto enemy ships, they had to be armed. Members of the Coast Guard mostly carry 9 mm pistols, M16 rifles, and shotguns.

During peacetime the Coast Guard helps keep our country safe. Missions at home are called Homeland Security missions. These missions include patrolling the harbors and waters that surround our country.

The Coast Guard is called a multi-mission service. That means it uses the same equipment for all of its jobs. Sailors carry guns when they board a ship that they think might be carrying drugs, just as during wartime. They also use the same large cutters and small patrol boats when they are out looking for smugglers, **terrorists**, and illegal immigrants.

Search-and-Rescue Missions

The Coast Guard also goes on search-and-rescue missions. It finds and rescues sailors in trouble or people who have fallen in the water. Most of the time, it uses boats to make a rescue. But in a big emergency when a boat is sinking or on fire, it uses a helicopter. The Coast Guard uses two kinds of helicopters: the HH65 Dolphin and the HH60J Jay Hawk. The helicopter crew pulls people from the water using a basket that is lowered by a cable.

Sometimes the Coast Guard uses a helicopter to rescue people from the water.

Soldiers through the Ages

A Continental Army soldier during the American Revolution

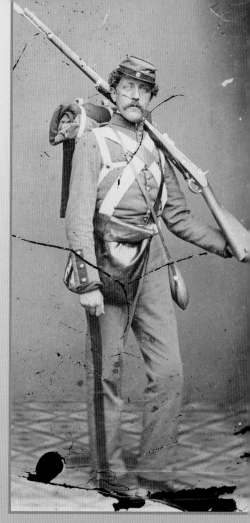

A Union Army enlisted soldier during the Civil War poses in full gear.

American soldiers from World War I are ready for a gas attack.

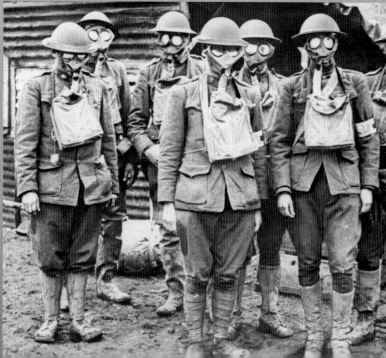

World War II
soldiers

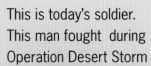
This is today's soldier.
This man fought during
Operation Desert Storm

American soldiers in Vietnam

Glossary

airborne carried in an aircraft; flying

aircraft carrier ship that carries planes and helicopters and has a place on deck for them to take off and land

ammunition materials that are fired from a weapon

branch small part of a larger organization

cockpit the area in the front of a plane where the pilot and copilot sit

combat fighting

communications means of exchanging information, for example, by radio, telephone, or e-mail

compass device that tells what direction a person is traveling

engineer person who designs bridges, tunnels, etc.

fatigues everyday military clothing or uniforms used on the job

fire-retardant material that can slow the spread of fire

free-fall fall through the sky without opening a parachute

grenade weapon that is filled with explosives and can be thrown or launched at a target

gunwale upper edge of a small or inflatable boat's side

hostile unfriendly

infiltrate sneak into enemy territory

inflate fill with air

insignia emblem or patch on a uniform

intelligence information about an enemy or an area

medic military medical personnel; someone who treats injuries

military having to do with war or the armed forces

navigate steer a vehicle or figure out where to go

paratrooper soldier trained and equipped to parachute from a plane

procedure way of doing things

reconnaissance search whose purpose is to obtain military information from or about the enemy

semiautomatic weapon in which ammunition is loaded at the same time that bullets already loaded are fired

shrapnel pieces of bombs, mines, or shells

sidearm small weapon, such as a pistol

small arm same as a sidearm

splint stiff piece of wood or plastic used to hold a broken bone in place

stealth working in secret

surveillance observing the enemy

tactical means of using forces in an action

terrorist person who uses violence to reach a goal

tourniquet something used to stop bleeding

volunteer person who does a job without being asked

More Books to Read

Abramovitz, Melissa. *The U.S. Navy at War*. Mankato, Minn.: Capstone Press, 2001.

Goldberg, Jan. *Green Berets: The U.S. Army Special Forces*. New York: Rosen Publishing Group, 2003.

Green, Michael. *The United States Coast Guard*. Mankato, Minn.: Capstone Press, 2000.

Hamilton, John. *Armed Forces*. Edina, Minn.: Abdo & Daughters, 2002.

Kennedy, Robert C. *Life As an Air Force Fighter Pilot*. Danbury, Conn.: Children's Press, 2000.

Kennedy, Robert C. *Life With the Navy Seals*. Danbury, Conn.: Children's Press, 2000.

Sawyer, Susan. *The Army in Action*. Berkeley Heights, N.J.: Enslow Publishers, Inc., 2001.

Index